ALSO BY ANNE MARIE MACARI

She Heads Into the Wilderness
Gloryland
Ivory Cradle

RED DEER | Anne Marie Macari

POEMS

A Karen & Michael Braziller Book | PERSEA BOOKS | New York

Persea Books, Inc.
277 Broadway
New York, NY 10007

Library of Congress Cataloging-in-Publication Data
Macari, Anne Marie.
[Poems. Selections]
Red deer : poems / Anne Marie Macari.—First edition.
      pages ; cm
ISBN 978-0-89255-456-0 (softcover: acid-free paper)
I. Title.
PS3563.A2335A6 2015
811'.54—dc23
      2014029883

First edition
Printed in the United States of America
Designed by Rita Lascaro

For Jerry

CONTENTS

Part One

All Souls   3

Paddling Upstream   5

Cave River   5

Labyrinth   6

Still Falling   8

Headlamp   9

Red Deer   10

Bison   11

Under Skin   12

The Meeting   13

Horse   15

Going Under   16

I Wore the Dress   18

Red Triangle   19

Falling Horse   20

Rain Legs   21

Rock Flesh   23

Part Two

Bone   27

Excavation, Rome   29

Pond   30

Unlit Corner   31

It Says   32

Rome, 2010   33

Fragment   35

Blue   36

Runaway   38

Emergency Room   39

Little Stick   40

42   Some Danger

43   Red Door

44   "They Are Dying As Numerously As Bees On A Harvest Day"

45   Teen Buried Alive For Talking To Boys

46   Zero

47   Red Cloak

49   Necropolis

Part Three

53   Neanderthal Flute

54   The Horse Wall

56   Black Line

57   Red Cord

58   Mammoth in Snow

60   The Sleeper's Every Breath

61   Swimming Reindeer on Mammoth Tusk

62   Missing

64   In The Flattened Grass of Sleep

65   Moth-Hinge

67   Solstice

68   Like Trees, Like Grass

69   Water Mill

70   Where the Hand Leads

72   Blue Hills

73   If I Could Walk

74   You Answer

75   After the Caves

76   Since There are Pockets

77   The Extinction of My Kind

78   Notes

80   Acknowledgements

PART ONE

If you stretch your hand, you touch the slope of the world . . .
Muriel Rukeyser

All Souls

Cougnac Cave, France

Many corners turned beneath
pencil-thin stalactites, thousands
like upside down candles,
wet flames dripping.
Beyond my mind's
violence, there,
an ibex painted
in calcite-milk
with wall-ooze for
a shaggy coat. Will it always
be buried? Memory
stumbling into mineral stillness,
crystallized, almost lucid, or carried—
a forgotten animal across
my shoulders, radiant
and awash in lactation, made
with hand, mouth, spit.
Dear friend, I remember
being painted
in coal and blood,
and the long gallery
where all souls parade.

Paddling Upstream

Leaving last slants of light.
Inside with the bats. Then sorry
when the light is gone. Sorry
to what stayed behind.
I call without a voice to the walls—
openings I can't see and keep
entering: sorry, sorry

Cave River

Alone, I left the visible world.
How hard my eyes pressed

but still no sight. Some things

abhor light and I almost
understand them growing

in their slime. I stayed
in darkness, stayed till

the winding sheet began to come

undone around me, all of me
loosening, separating, even

the pieces of my own spine
unhooked, and bits of me

floating off with the river—arm

ear   teeth—the cave a throat
swallowing me. Later, it spit me up,

thrust me out like a boat—

my body returning to me—light
that picked my pieces up

and made of me
what it could.

Labyrinth

and painted onto my inner

skull, pigment
blown through bone,

your voice, blown through,
your handprint

inside my skull

*

In that labyrinth got lost

and the thousands
of old lives

herds, so quiet

*

Only paint on rock
only sandstone lamps,
ash-boats

*

Earth's phantom limb—

under-heaven
hung with slick calcite

moonmilk

*

Tallow lamp, tooth
in the rock, can't see them

running along the walls

How did you come here?
In a dream I fell

through a hole in the earth

Still Falling

Remember being dressed in
the fur of earth, our loping

limbs? Once I dreamed
of you falling, and I fell

after you, but there was nothing
to land on and I woke up.

And then I wondered if you
were still there, locked

in the dream, still falling,
but without me to find you.

We can't count on waking,
and if we did wake, opening our

eyes, our backs against
the tough grass, and if we lifted

our hands, what strange
animals would they be?

Headlamp

Carrying little, wearing a weak
headlamp, a mile in, stumbling
and wet, the cave walls
like my own insides and I an animal
painted there. Darkness
filling in my cartoon lines, my blank self.

I am inside a hole
in the earth, with pots
of ochre and ash. My offerings—
your hair, the print of my hand.

Red Deer

Covalanas Cave, Spain

Once I was an animal, like you, red deer,
bright as arterial blood, with

sure feet. The painter pressed you
to life with pointer and thumb.

Your one eye and pert ears.
Now you leap inside me, over

and over from my cliff
of trapped air. Back legs tucked.

Red, red, the female creatures grazing inside—
green and in motion, the earth below.

Bison

To become the rock, and then
the bison of the rock, hunched where
the stone hunches, there to cure myself,

unhook the human worm. To live
where the primordial river rushed,
old dry bed, old eyes in the dark.

Mouth of stone, open for me.
Painter, swipe the charcoal torch
against my brain.

Under Skin

Under skin and into the entrances.
Like someone tracing the rock-ledge
of my clavicle, peering into
my windy sockets. Secrets, letters
written inside, never sent, scrawled
like the script of my brain—so I have kept

my mistakes to myself, hoarded guilt,
hoarded joy too. I should have turned
toward you once more, just once
for us to meet again in this world.
In the painted cave of my mind

you are there—the grace of you—how
I've taken your image inside me,
with all my tenderness I keep you—
little horse, little deer.

The Meeting

From silver,
from water collecting

like an eye, dripping
through rock,

the pool sings,
it widens then blinks.

Some things rise
and some things sink.

I can feel the hardness
giving way, and water

entering me, I wait

for you to float
on top of me.

Slow crystal melt,
well of mineral sweat.

I think years pass,
decades while

you look through me
as if I'm not here.

The water pools, sings.

It widens, blinks.
Some things rise

and some things sink.
And some things

come to me
to drink.

Horse

Candamo Cave, Spain

High up the wall you seemed to move
in the fatty lamplight—
your short legs and erect mane

and in the grasslands a sea of you
How you fell
How you tasted

Tell me the story of when first
I held you   femur to flank
miles we raced one body

the wind splayed around us   How
you let me ride any direction
Lips pulled back   snorting

How you wore me   clinging
my legs raw   the marriage
long and lonely   Runaway

Going Under

The meat inside the earth is packed
material, though sometimes there's space,
an opal darkness where a river underground
once gouged tunnels and rooms,
a dry bed where I passed a hardened waterfall,
passed mineral flowers and slick pillars growing
drop by sticky drop—the life of darkness
mushrooming, foaming underground.
Darkness can't burn out, it makes
an unseen glow, like a coal waiting
to be lit. Buried life, I've
gone under. How did I think that light
was everything when here it only
outlines the intelligence
of the dark: discs fallen across
boulders like slices of moon,
memory walls and spinning columns.
I went into the opal dark, I held
my wild shadow for comfort.
I could have kept going but I was afraid
to burn out where my eyes
would be useless. Though some things
live in no-light, I cannot.
I could have stayed, wandering
through the holes in the world,
but there were voices, sounds
of dripping, and one way back climbing
slippery thresholds, trying to imagine again
the open sky, my old life just
a dream, one way back climbing
toward a hole where the rock

was crusted over, curtained with ferns,
and the lit world came seeping in.

I Wore the Dress

I wore the dress inside
my body, draping

what couldn't be seen.
A dress, flowing.

Spun the thread myself from silk and iron.
A spindle rolled along the thigh.

Needle from a bird bone.
Write to me and send

me books. I want to know
botany: umbels, spikes,

clusters, the lipped or hooded—
shadows under petals, shadows

where the pink uplifts.
Dressing, waiting through days of rain,

floorboards coughing,
a gentleness with membranes,

a guardian, garden,
a dress inside

my body, draping
what couldn't be seen.

Red Triangle

When I was joy I woke
with the smear on my legs

and we painted the red
triangle. Since then I can't count

all the times I've died.
Warm nights the singing

so full it swallows me,
I can't hear my own dreams for all

the calls, all the sucklings
wild for earth's milk.

I was born with this wound,
it bleeds it bleeds it bleeds

Falling Horse

Ochre, and the black line
of mane painted soft on the wall, legs
pointing up. Who knows how
to fall without landing, to pass through
each dimension upside down? Forgotten,
the upper world and all that light.

Why do you haunt me?
For a little while I want to be alone
with the animals, with the cold stone
and my lamp. The black mane
caresses the horse's head,
floating between us.

Rain Legs

Rain walks long miles.
A soft milky rain

to fatten the calf and soothe
the mother.

Rain strides the ranges and seas.
Its footprint makes lakes,

if it kneels, a river.

From a great distance I see
rain legs coming.

Some message, urgent,
someone rain wants to meet.

Once my eyes were cinder,
my teeth fell out, once

I was tied to a stake,
burning, left

to die.   Just to walk free

on rain legs, that's all
I ask. From a great distance

a herd of rain, I call out to
the trees and flowers, get ready,

open your mouths.

Rock Flesh

*"Water dripping from these stalactites
is from a rain during World War II."*
Guide, Cougnac Cave, Sept., 2010

As if this cave had glands, its tapered
hollows dripping, earth
trying out its forms here—alien
and bulbous, disordered, cracked.
I feel how close crystal
is to flesh, just a membrane or two
apart. How the old rain can
pass through the bodies
of the dead, through
bone and bedrock
and not taste of rot or terror, pooling
in the belly, sweating
all down the walls. How
the porous limestone leaks
its eggshell glaze
like some bird
birthing, without sun
or wind, but in a cavernous
womb, crystal growing
its calculated pace. Maybe I was born
through strands of memory,
maybe I drank mud. Maybe I have filtered
like rain through unending bodies. Close,
close to rock flesh I feel here
and to the rain that fell before
this life, dripping on my hair.

PART TWO

There are things down there still coming ashore.
Never make the mistake of thinking life is now
adjusted for eternity. It gets into your head—the
certainty, I mean—the human certainty, and then
you miss it all . . .

Loren Eisley

Bone

I know what it's like to dig
    but not find the bone
        you are looking for. Buried

deep and tight as a knuckle
    beneath the garbage
        and rubble. If the tongue

had a bone, or if breasts
    had artifacts buried
        inside, beyond the milk

and ducts. If the eye had
    the bone of sight locked
        in its black interior,

old bone secretly given.
    I step down onto the ancient
        street of brick houses,

so many bricks they tint
    the dark air. In the dead
        city sleeping ash stirs

its powdery afterlife—
    I have reached deep
        I have turned my eyes away

so what I look for might find me,
    take shape in my hand,
        earth slashed down

to the bone, fingers scooping
black dirt, my whole arm
reaching inside.

Excavation, Rome

Water rushes behind the walls,
I hear it pulse, threatening to flood through.
How deep to go, past unearthed
mosaics, urns, painted
birds, the way lit where
small bristles touched
each memory scar then
grain by grain swept
the holes clear.
And this last room, scraped
clean again as when they lived here,
water springing into
the house through an ancient pipe.
Bright liquid, unbreakable,
playing off the thin bricks
then draining out of sight.

Pond

Wheeling night voices across
the field, rolling up the trees—
trills and grunts from fetid mud,
a watery membrane
where once I broke through
to a miasma of tiny wings, a wavering
green light below. Where is the pond
I swam in, where my puffing gills, ripe
airless muck, my brackish element—
I leave the table, candles walking
the wind, I stand inside the chanting,
a landed animal, helpless.

Unlit Corner

Raking winter's spoils, heat blooming.
Rain's loosened the undersoil and the thick
dead leaves—lost months

in the debris. I dig and plant but something
still surrounds me, some old blanket leftover
from the cold, some unlit corner—

fluency in the black soil, the clumps
releasing, earthy stench
in the voices, broken, rising

It Says

I know you are there, I can hear you
in the soles of my feet.

Sleeping, curled to make a home
with my spine,

my flesh making that orphan music
it makes for you,

someone within hums
or whines all night, all

the witnesses gone, you, gone
from yourself.

Talk to me, you are the ear
of my longing, talk

to me, that's
all the body wants, all it ever says.

Rome, 2010

Here where slabs have fallen and wild caper and fig
grow out of the cracks, I wander the city, the strange body,

does each one who lived here leave an empty space,

are there leopards
dreaming below the coliseum where winches

once hoisted caged
animals and men, does the spectator-animal
still abide here, in his element?

Leopards and leopards, leopards, leopards and leopards, dream-
running across the arena

                              *

Failure moves with me, I cross the river to circle the old
prison looking for some sign.   No plaque where he was arrested,

no trail from Rome to Fossoli
to Auschwitz and back.   Remember he said

the saddest times in the camps

were the rare days without work, no marching in freezing mud, dogs
barking—rare minutes when life came rushing back—

                              *

Trap doors, blood on the floor—

Rooms vast and deep.   How they fill the holes
with rubble. What's stacked beneath to hold up
the flying arches?

Crowds of ghosts at the monuments, thin as parchment, words scrawled

across the pages of their skin, streets filling, emptying.   From the hiding
places, small figs, wild growing

Fragment

Carved stone
in the dirt   broken

but whole   more beautiful

I can only give you what's left—
Hand   eyelid   tooth

My head   on your chest   dreaming
The rest of me   already gone

Blue

Sometimes no softness given: the last
cuff of brown leaves, roots

like brittle wires in rocky ground,
moss-fur stiffening in the creases.

Out my window for years, the same
woodpecker drilling

as the tree turned skeletal, bare.
I stand before the window

to listen for the sound
of your crossing—how a tree

can become a lake, or how
a body in illness can take

a gorge inside itself
as if to say there is space

even inside the dying
and inside space, more space,

unmeasured, so when you were ready
you could slip like an egg

from your shell, *pass away,*
falling still in your swaddling

clothes, still in the grass,
felled, though all around you

things vibrated, shivered.
Unmeasured space: how close

we came: the edge shimmering
in your eyes, blue gorge

into which you fell.

Runaway

And I answer from where
the bunched grass is between us.

From the red herd painted alive
on the rocks, from

falling horse. Can't stop moving,
even in the dream, up and down

the stairs with nothing to wear but
pale blue and one shoe missing.

Leave me something in chalk
or charcoal, flint or fur,

I'll come through
your hands. With you

always.

When I go, the points
of the star send me

every direction.

Emergency Room

Blue thread of the monitor rising
and falling, someone's blood

splattered on the wall.
If I stopped talking to you

who would I be? I leaned
into the plastic-covered bed,

leaned into something I can't
explain and felt wellness sewn

into me. I don't mean
the small pills, the cup of water.

Here in this curtained
bit of space, this scarred

container, they touch me
kindly, 1 AM, and I am traveling

two places at once

Little Stick

And what is this moving stick, this
old wood of the body.

Enter through the wooden door
across the chest,

sit before the hearth that pumps
a bit too fast.

Stick of life, you are getting older,
so grainy and the corners

of your mouth are dragged down, even
deranged. Be still,

little stick, there is no more scraping
and polishing, there are fish eyes

and walking. Old tendrils around
the neck. The wreath of the mind

circling, circling. A dropper of food.
Let blossom be inside the bone

where no one knows, all the pink
vessels. And let this be

the age of the stick,
rough, twisted, a work

of art, with a small flair, flaw,
in the twirl of its spine.

Some Danger

The many hymens of skin and air,
torn, will leave their stain. If we

touch. But I can keep
my desperateness from you, and you

can keep your outline, the silhouette,
with the light behind you, it

is beautiful like that, flared with pink
and orange around your head.

Even from such distance, pollination,
some danger. What makes

us swallow ourselves and roll
in the powder of desire?

I am here, waiting to break down.

Red Door

Then I was open and empty
and from the place
he had passed through
blood foamed. I still see
her gloved hand reaching inside—

pain so bad they held me down.
Even now, blocking my path,
her hand on my red door.

"They Are Dying as Numerously as Bees on a Harvest Day"

(letter to the Lord Lt. of Ireland, 1847)

Quiet as cloth folding. Who once light was,
with eyes speaking. Sweet, you become *you,*

a veil of flesh, throbbing membrane
like a baby's head. So blessed I am

to touch that flesh, hold that hand.
Now the door is ajar

Teen Buried Alive for Talking to Boys

Stop the pulsing and singing, gag
the hairy mouth. To dust and dirt
go back. Minerals, film her eyes,
her tongue, coat the streams
of her lungs. Shovels, slice and fill
the air around her. Chickens
scratch and flail. Girl, why
were you born with that hole?

Zero

All night, sleep—a pit
I crawled into—deep inside

the oblivious black seed,
oval eye. Sleep

the down being—and why
should I come back from that zero?

You knew me but you didn't know
my zero, hole

I disappear through,
hole that I am.

Red Cloak

I've traveled from

milk to milk   squatting over
nothing

the left and right sides

hinged together at the neck
left lobe and right lobe

left breast   right breast

and across the ribs' scaffolding
knots and loops

making a spine

my body
my valley inside—

my sex gulf—
turn with me

I am wanting
to be opened

up the middle   I am wanting

to part the inner fur
inside the cloak

Don't think me strange
when I have been

preparing all my life

to be simple   a red
parting from cunt to chin

a road   and everything
pouring in

Necropolis

Beneath St. Peter's Basilica, Rome

In the fossil city—amber light, stacked urns,
doorways to duck under—an old buried street,
bricks and mortar holding two thousand years,
so much brick the red air is always twilight. I'm deep
in the spoils, in rubble far beneath
the great dome. Here, the dead
have been dragged from their houses
and purged. I've moved
underground into corners
where the river after rain laps up
through dirt, through bone and flesh. Sometimes
I'm running from the sky,
sickened, wanting a little blindness
while I unlearn my myths.
I have been wrong—some love
given rightly, some relic
of myself rightly given—
On the false
altar inside,
where I believed
and embellished the old stories
I want to place something
simple, made by my hands,
without worship, for no one
to find. I've tried to climb
down, through the painted doors, as though
the floor would open, merciful, into a pool
of memory, sheltered by the dead city
while I learn to know the animal

of myself, how to touch
the world, unshamed
in impossible red twilight,
thresholds all crossing.

PART THREE

There was a day
when all the animals talked to me

Anne Sexton

Neanderthal Flute

Foraging in roots, in labyrinths where
trees spoke scraping each other in wind
I never thought of myself
as separate from my skin, without
whorled fingertips, without lips.

For the experiments boring into me,
for the drills, for whatever makes me
useful now. If not
useful, then beautiful—fossil pollen
spilled over me.   Open

the memory room slowly
put the singing bone
to my mouth

The Horse Wall

Cap Blanc, France

I ate stone, entered it, my hand
reaching to nudge the horse
through the wall, stroke it out, carving
horse eye and velvet ear, massaging

up and down muscled legs.
So many springs now of cracking ice, thaw
taking me down—a thousand walls
between us and I can't rub through.

I fall apart and can't speak past
the carbon in my mouth,
the pebbles. Are you still
following the herd? Was it real—

how I ate stone and walked
through a galaxy shining
in the flecks, found
space no one else could see. Found

you waiting there. You
who opened my stone body.
Who softened my sadness. Now,
I never want to be touched, never

again be touched, all
the groping hands
and pickaxes, all the stars
of distance dancing madly—

My bludgeoned animal,
there was a place tender
in rock where first
you showed yourself.

There your soul-eye,
soul-eye that nothing
can remove, black space
in the wall of the world.

Black Line

Angles-sur-Anglin, France

Where families slept and built
their fires against the limestone wall
animals move out of rock: lion, horse, ibex,
and in the center three women, sculpted,
one belly marked with the dark
line of pregnancy,
the birthing out through
muscle and stone, fur
to fur, dark
pigment of the belly and hairy
thatch—yes, I see now,
I see us tunneling through, time
and again. Animals
on their haunches or
looking over their shoulders.
Oh, if only we saw them
painted in the dark, etched
or sculpted, if only we stopped
to look and rubbed our fingers
along their bodies. Long the birthing, bones
forced open, the tunnel taking us,
our gyrations against
wet walls, life
pushed out, sent on, sent on.
We don't know
if we are alive—stone,
air, flesh—what borders
did we cross?

Red Cord

She who held the thread,
deep in, off-center
inside the soft body

of rock, drew me in.
How would I find my way back?
Outside, grasses bent, bright

wind. Inside, the rock's
oval opening, red cord
beating

Mammoth in Snow

Rouffignac—Cave of a Hundred Mammoths

Ice clinks along strands of matted
hair, ice in my breathing. We are frozen
as far as we can see, a trail
across thousands of years, thousands
of winters in this bone-world.
This knowing is just a flash, a vortex,
as if a hawk would spiral
down instead of skyward and open
a pit in the earth and into it
I would fall, tipped
off my path. Maybe
I'm falling now
the sky moving farther from me
and I in a cold heap.
Snow against
snow, walls of dreams
and projections, a turning
toward private singing,
toward strings in my throat
and the tender tip
of my trunk, stroking. When I
am just an image I'll wander all through
the long torrent-scoured tunnels, along walls
of moonmilk and into the crawling space
where with one hand moving fast
she paints me on the ceiling
and I'm alive again with
many herds: leapers, stampeders,
lonely stragglers. Snow mounds
like a soul over me—I huddle,

a massive beast
confused in the whiteout.

The Sleeper's Every Breath

For hours—no—for days, heavy snow. Tunnels
could be dug through it into the woods and the mind

could hide out there. Snow builds and gathers and the arms
of the trees bear it night and day as if no stillness

could ever be enough. Now the sleeper's every breath
hardens under the freeze. Crystal shroud, white lace—a spark

of ice began once inside me, remember?

Swimming Reindeer on Mammoth Tusk

Muscular, the creases
of their ribs still pumping.
Nipples hard, ears flat
and the great antlers falling
almost like hair across their backs.
I will never see how their bulk
presses the current, only
this carving two hands made,
swift lines across their coats,
eyes forward and bulging, male
behind female. They keep
swimming—no end, no rising
through stalks to follow
the tundra north.   Some things
have been tamed in me
and my skin grows strange.
Sometimes I cannot
grasp you, wild memory. The lost,
so beautiful, caught in it
up to their nostrils.
Where is their trail?
My torso grows heavier,
how will I swim?
Who will be behind me? Where
is the muddy bank?

Missing

Long stretches in my ghost canyon, in
my lower fields, long stretches

aimless in the house, climbing stairs,
cleaning—trying to make things right.

Once in a cave's narrow passage the light

flashed on the wall and a single hand
glowed back: hand

of 40,000 years, near where Neanderthals

starved in frozen Spain.   I believe in
the sacred hand of all species: bird

hand or mouse, or mark of the parasite.

Everyday less sure of how to be
in this brown world—

                        *

Burn me, burn my body, don't leave anything
to chance.   *My letter to the world:*

don't look for me. Darling, don't ask
me to sleep beside your coffin, side

by side up there on Mt. Hope—why

take up room?   On the radio a scientist says—
I have to live with that—

40,000 elephants culled—for ecology.   *The biggest*
mistake of my life.

There are giant holes dug into
cave floors, I've seen some—

where Cave Bears slept out the long Ice Age
winters, sometimes a fossil

skeleton where a bear never woke up—

What if I could go down into a bear's old
hollow, if I could smell

its dreams, reach inside extinct ribs?

Already there's something in me
that will kill me, but what

would it mean to flourish?

In the Flattened Grass of Sleep

Layers of years as one now, you appear—
mineral eyes, paws planted beside
my shoulders, saliva glistening,
your breath rank and bloody.

Leave your scent on me and the wide
savannah of your stride, stalk me
out of myself, furred, clawed—a yellow
terror flashing through grass.

Moth-Hinge

Just as well fall from the sky,
just as well become

the body of a moth
with wings a touch

can tear. And no importance.
And the battering moth

that tried to get in, and the festering
cocoon, and the eggs, and the eggs

and the tissue paper wings.

The air fills with dust—
something crushed against a window,

transparency of body
unfolding in the last moment.

For you I became a nest—

silken home of membrane and milk—
a hinge opening. Once

I was afraid of everything. Now
the womb's cavern

closes and I see through thin wings—
all the world tinged

with that bloody light.

Wherever you fly across the falling
earth, wherever your touch

makes the air move, my dust
is on you. What I have given

is what I am. What is gone from me
fills me. My moth-

hinge, under which—I don't know—

earth-bed, cradle—
your dust on me, mine on you.

Solstice

Green the bellows of the trees,
green where the horses lowered
their heads to eat, green the thin
inch worm that hung by a thread
from my hair

green the beginnings, clustered
at the tip of the stem and what tried
to pry it open, scum slipping
the surface of the pond

and even the sun, stained by too much green.
Long, long day of light,
stay, be the scorch
in my mind, let me wander
between the twin discs, undivided.

Cresting hurts me, that hollow
under the arc and the solid eye
of light coming over the top,
hovering before it starts to fall,

then what calm, a sky that lingers,
the grass cools,
the horses wander into the basin
still eating, forgetting us—

in blue light I walk home, spare
calls ringing from the woods

Like Trees, Like Grass

The multitudes of the invisible hum
around us, inside too, they speak
in code, busy making things, the sheen

of their milk filling the atmosphere--
water and sky speaking to each other.
I awaken for a day and stumble

into the middle of my life, the ones
I love wandering near me, not noticing
how alive I am, how much milk

I've absorbed, like the trees, like
grass, sated and full, the tidal pull
of days rushes out before me, so clear now,

and the pale eye slips away—

Water Mill

Rafters dusted in flour. With
a lever, a small movement, grain
sluices overhead and down the chute.
I am anxious to part the fine white dust in the air,
like a river, and find myself
in milky haze, light catching

the floaters. He ties the bag
of flour with a string, shows me

the mill's wheel. I want to go down
to the wheel and the water, or leave
a hand print on a wooden beam.
I am writing you without
pen or paper, crushed powder sifting
down on me, bread-dust.

Where the Hand Leads

I follow—hand on the doorknob,
hand extended from

the shoulder, from down behind
the wing of the aching blade. There

in my back, the hand's root.
Late at night the hand moves

to undress me—buttons, bra, hand
twisted behind, just toward

the pain itself. So much reaching,

for what? And the strawberry of pain
fading, losing its color.   Some moments

all life, all the words

of my mouth pass through my fingers
and I am open-palmed, eyes

closed, feeling the sponge of space.
Out there, a pouring,

fingertips far gone from the body
making their way around porous walls—

oh the maze I ago, long time,
entered, and the hand

quiet, out ahead

Blue Hills

Even silence has a voice, it rests
heavy in my mouth and paints

my ribcage silver. Inside, a nest

where heart and lungs almost brush
each other. All night

my mouth opens to exchange
one emptiness for another;

with flesh it is like that, with all things:

the thankful dirt, thankful trees,
bent summer light.

If I Could Walk

through space
as the night sky
wanders inside

the earth, oh please,
my four legs
free, entering you, you

entering me

You Answer

I know there is a trail, stained, and clues to lead me down
into charcoal: spoils of fossils where I am buried, piles

of bones, all of us—antlers, vertebrae, jaws. Where
they measure a pelvis, analyze the rings

of a chipped tooth. Where you answer through

rock and water
surprising me

in the black strata—

We are folded in

deep in the honeycomb, my liquid ear
oozing, letting go

old loops of failure.   A trail down
into charcoal and charged dust

through splinters and shards—

my layers, my shields—

you answer, surprising me
in the black strata

After the Caves

Restless, I want to return and stand
at the mouth, where wild fig trees
grow from rock canopy, and watch
clouds sweep above grasslands,
no herds, just a solitary road
winding below. I want to lean
backwards at the cave's threshold
where the cool opening meets
the sun's heat, called
in both directions, behind me
the branching tunnels, stalagmites
like great solid dreams. Living
on the surface I dream of caves—
my animal walking among mineral
accretions, my memory
coated with lucid calcite—each day
slicked onto the pillar
of my body. For now, I'm being awakened
to these holes in the earth,
I'm learning the gape within, how
the earth feels inside
its tender chambers.
Somewhere there is a room
I am crawling towards.

Since There Are Pockets

Since there are pockets
in space, and warp,
a mind that can't see itself,
and there the wolf skulls

are buried, and the elk horn,
the jaw of a bear—we placed
our hands just so on the walls
of space so you would know

we were here

The Extinction of My Kind

When the carcass
of the mind takes off
its bloody coat and wanders
toward its life again

I come back from my ancient sleep,
I come back on all fours
and stand and drag my claws
down rock and mud

leaving signs for you, I come back,
lumbering into the cold, light-blinded,
I come back. The earth
is shining but the place

without light pulses
inside me. I come
back to you. *Dear friend,*
I slept so long I went into

my animal body, I longed
for you there

NOTES

Many of these poems were written in response to caves I visited in Belize, France, and Spain. The caves in France and Spain were for the most part sites with Ice Age cave art; art that was between 12,000 and 40,000 years old. The art included cave paintings and engravings, rock shelters with sculpted friezes, and much portable art from that time period such as female figures, animal carvings, pendants, as well as many tools. Any sites mentioned in the poems are sites I have visited. For visits to Ice Age caves in Northern Spain and in France I am indebted to the guidance and expertise of Paul Bahn, archaeologist and writer.

Red Triangle: In some decorated caves there are painted red triangles. Their central points are facing the ground and they often have a line up the middle, the common interpretation is that they represent vulvas.

Falling Horse: Refers to a painted upside down horse in Lascaux.

Pond: "Wavering green light" comes from Loren Eisley's book *The Immense Journey.*

Rome, 2010: for Nissim Alhadeff, 1918–2009.

Necropolis: A Necropolis from the first century AD lies buried beneath the Basilica of St. Peter's and has now been partially unearthed. The original purpose of the excavation was to prove the legend that the altar of the Basilica was built above the grave of St. Peter—in other words as directed by the Vatican they were looking for St. Peter's bones. In the process what they found was a city of the dead, with streets and decorated "houses" built to hold individuals and families in sarcophagi and urns.

Blue is in memory of Bruce Coe, 1930–2009.

"They Are Dying As Numerously As Bees On A Harvest Day": Is taken from the Memorial for the Irish Famine in lower Manhattan and is also in memory of Bruce Coe.

The Horse Wall: Refers to a rock shelter in the Dordogne that was partly destroyed in the early 20th century by men digging with pick axes who finally saw the horses sculpted into the rock (c. 15,000 years ago) and stopped, though by then much damage had already been done. In front of the great sculpted frieze a grave was also found holding the skeleton of a paleolithic woman. "Studies suggest that the artist was left-handed, and the skeleton displays strong musculature on that side." There is only one other known site "with a burial in front of a decorated panel."

(Paul Bahn, Cave Art, A Guide to the Decorated Ice Age Caves of Europe, Frances Lincoln Limited, 2012).

Swimming Reindeer on Mammoth Tusk: This small carving, "The Swimming Reindeer" (c. 13,000 years), can be found in The British Museum.

ACKNOWLEDGEMENTS

Versions of these poems have appeared in following magazines:

The American Poetry Review: Going Under, The Meeting, Since There are Pockets, Under Skin

The Cortland Review: Mammoth in Snow

Field: Labyrinth, All Souls

Five AM: Black Line, Swimming Reindeer

Five Points: The Horse Wall

The Great River Review: Bison, After the Caves, Red Cloak, Red Deer, Red Triangle

Gris Gris: Headlamp, Bone

The Massachusetts Review: Little Stick

Miramar: Moth-Hinge, Necropolis

Poetry International: Still Falling, It Says, Rock Flesh

Terminus: Cave River, Horse

World Literature Today: Neanderthal Flute, The Extinction of My Kind

I would like to thank The Virginia Center for the Arts and the MacDowell Colony for time, space, and solitude—rare gifts.

I would also like to thank Gabriel Fried and everyone at Persea for believing in this book.

For their wisdom and kindness I'm always and ever grateful to Jan Heller Levi, Joan Larkin, and Jean Valentine. Thank you also to dear friends Jane Mead and Judith Vollmer for support and insight. And to my family, Jerry, Noah, Luke, Jeremy, my mother and father, all of you give me so much.